Acknowledgements

I want to thank my family: Dan, Lexi, Isaac, Sydney and Jude for forging this journey to New Zealand with me. I also want to thank my amazing online community for taking the time to watch, comment, and help us on our journey to New Zealand!

If you want to follow along on our journey check out
my YouTube channel
@Kiwiamericans

I would love to see how these recipes have turned out in your kitchen! Tag me @Kiwiamericans across social.

Kia Ora,

I am so excited to bring my kitchen to yours and share some of my favourite American recipes with my New Zealand Whānau. I have adapted these recipes to the New Zealand/Australian kitchen in terms of ingredients used, ingredient names and temperatures. Thank you all for sharing with me what recipes you would love to see.

If you don't know us, we are a family of 6 who moved from the USA to NZ in 2013. I love sharing our journey on social media and I am definitely changing as a person from living in a new culture and seeing how to really embrace balance and enjoy the stunning nature that New Zealand provides. I have spent the last few years building an amazing online community on TikTok and YouTube who requested this book. This is my labour of love for all that my community has given me!

I truly hope this recipe book brings some amazing treats into your home! Please let me know what you think of it and what you would like to see in the next recipe book. I am thinking the next recipe book shall be a baking book with items such as: snickerdoodles, angel food cake, buckeyes etc.

Please email me at kiwiamericansnz@gmail.com and let me know what you think of this book and post pictures of your creations on Instagram @kiwiamericans.

Enjoy!

Tara Hulbert
Kiwiamericans.com

Welcome to my kitchen!

Table of Contents

Pumpkin Pie - page 5
Sloppy Joe - page 7
Chocolate Chip Cookies - page 9
Banana Bread - page 11
Bruschetta - page 13
Buttermilk Pancakes - page 15
Peanut Butter Cookies - page 17
Real "Philly" cheesesteak - page 19
American Chilli - page 21
Cornbread - page 23
Deep Dish "Chicago" style pizza - page 25
Cherry Pie - page 27
Chicken Enchilada - page 29
American Cheeseburger - page 31
Buttermilk Biscuits and Gravy - page 33
Meatloaf - page 35
Buttermilk Ranch Dressing - page 37

Pumpkin pie is a staple at Thanksgiving in America. Having 5-6 pumpkin pies at a large gathering is not unusual. Americans are a bit obsessed with pumpkin spice products in the Fall. (which I love of course) Thanksgiving falls in November every year, which is Fall in the USA. Depending on where you live in the USA, Fall is known for football, leaves falling, and pumpkin/apple farms!

Pumpkin Pie

Recipe is on the back of the Pumpkin Puree from an American store (Libby's is the best!)

Ingredients:

- 3/4 cup of sugar
- 1/2 tsp salt
- 1 tsp ground cinnamon
- 1/2 tsp ginger
- 1/4 tsp cloves or nutmeg
- 2 large eggs
- 1 can pumpkin purée (or you can make your own pumpkin puree with fresh pumpkin)
- 1 can of evaporated milk
- 1 pie crust (store bought or see recipe)

Watch me make this recipe on YouTube: @Kiwiamericans

Directions

Mix all ingredients in one bowl and pour into pie crust. Bake at 220 C for 15 min and 180 C for 30-40 minutes. Serve with whip cream! Note: You cannot freeze this pie.

Butter crust recipe - this makes 2 pie crusts but I only used one in the video
- 2 1/2 cups of all purpose flour
- 1 cup butter
- 1 teaspoon salt
- 6-8 TBL ice water

Mix top 4 ingredients together and then slowly add the water that you need to make the crust mix but not too sticky. Put in the refrigerator for 30 min before use. Freeze the extra crust to use another time.

You may be wondering where "Sloppy Joe" got its name? You won't be after you try this recipe! The sandwich is quite "sloppy" to eat with meat falling out every which way. Sloppy Joe is a popular food for children in America. You will find this served at most school cafeterias and at many potluck gatherings as it feeds a crowd!

Sloppy Joe

Ingredients:

- 1 kg Beef or pork mince (the best is a bit of both)
- 1 onion
- 1 capsicum (pepper) any color
- 2 cloves garlic
- 2 tsp chilli powder
- 1/4 cup brown sugar
- salt and pepper
- 1/3 cup of ketchup (depending on how much mince)
- 1tsp cayenne pepper (optional)

Directions

Brown the meat. Take out any extra fat from the meat before adding the rest of the ingredients. Add onion, garlic and capsicum to the meat and cook for 2 min. Add the remaining ingredients and let it simmer for 5-10 minutes. Enjoy!

Watch me make this recipe on YouTube@ kiwiamericans

In New Zealand, many biscuits (cookies) are hard and crunchy but this cookie recipe is soft, chewy, moist... simply the best.

The **BEST** Chocolate Chip Cookie recipe!

Ingredients:

- 115g (½ cup) butter unsalted
- 115g (½ cup) margarine or butter substitute - any kind will work!
- ¾ cup of brown sugar
- ¾ cup of white sugar
- 1 egg
- 1 tsp vanilla
- 2 ½ cups flour
- 1 tsp baking soda
- ½ tsp salt
- 1 ½ cups of chocolate chips

Directions

Preheat the oven to 180 degrees C. Cream butter and sugars together. Add egg and vanilla to the mix. Add dry ingredients. Stir in chocolate chips. Bake for 8 min 30 sec and let them continue to bake on the cookie sheet after you take them out of the oven for an additional 5 min. *I am quite serious about this baking time - trust me!*

Adjust the time based on how hot your oven gets. The cookies should be a golden brown. Ummm...you're welcome ;)

I have seen banana bread in NZ, but I have not seen chocolate chip banana bread. This is a typical recipe in the Midwest to bring to a potluck or to a friend who is feeling sick. Great for lunchboxes!

Chocolate Chip Banana Bread

Ingredients:

(2 loaves or 1 big loaf)
- 2 ½ cups flour
- 1 tsp baking soda
- ¾ tsp salt
- 1 ¼ cups sugar
- ½ cup oil (I use vegetable oil)
- 3 eggs
- 1 ½ cup of mashed ripe bananas (3 large)
- 1 cup of chocolate chips

Directions

Preheat the oven to 190 degrees C.
Grease/line pans. In a small bowl, mix flour, baking soda and salt. In a large bowl, beat on medium speed with an electric mixer the sugar, oil, and eggs until blended. Add bananas and beat on low speed. Add flour mixture. Stir in chocolate chips. Pour into pans and bake for 30-40 min until the knife comes out clean.

I have had some really great and some really bad Bruschetta in New Zealand. I love this recipe as it has the freshest ingredients. This will definitely be a crowd-pleaser at your next party if you want to impress your guests, this bruschetta recipe will definitely impress!

Bruschetta

Ingredients:

- 2 TBL Olive Oil
- 5 cloves of fresh garlic finely minced
- 2 pints of grape tomatoes cut in half (best if you can get ones in multiple colours)
- 1TBL balsamic Vinegar
- Fresh basil leaves
- Salt/pepper to taste
- 1 package Feta cheese
- French Baguette
- 5-6 TBL butter

Directions

Add everything to a large bowl and combine (except bread/butter). It is best to let this sit in the fridge for a few hours before guests arrive. Even overnight works well.

Cut the baguette diagonally and cook it in butter on a skillet. Flip over and brown the other side. Add more butter as needed. Spoon the tomato mixture onto the hot bread. Top with feta cheese and serve immediately.

Pikelets were a new idea for me when I moved to New Zealand as they were surprisingly small pancakes. In the USA, we like big, fluffy, buttermilk pancakes. My family adds blueberry or chocolate chips right into the batter. Other toppings we love on our pancakes are real maple syrup, powdered sugar, mixed berries and whipped cream!

Buttermilk Pancakes

Ingredients:

- ¾ cup milk
- 2 TBL white vinegar
- 1 cup all-purpose flour
- 2 TBL white sugar
- 1 tsp baking powder
- ½ tsp baking soda
- ½ tsp salt
- 1 egg
- 1 tsp of vanilla or almond extract
- 2 TBL butter (melted)
- Cooking spray

Directions

Combine milk and vinegar in a medium bowl and set aside for 5 minutes to "sour" (homemade buttermilk). Combine flour, sugar, baking powder, baking soda and salt in a large mixing bowl.

Whisk egg and butter into "soured" milk. Pour the flour mixture into the wet ingredients and whisk until the lumps are gone. Heat a skillet and coat with cooking spray. Pour ¼ cup of batter onto the skillet and cook until bubbles appear on the surface. (This is also an excellent time to add your chocolate chips or blueberries!) Flip over until golden brown on the other side. Make sure that they are cooked all the way through and enjoy!

Other toppings we love on our pancakes are some real maple syrup, powdered sugar, mixed berries and whipped cream!

Americans love their peanut butter! Peanut butter is excellent in baking as it makes desserts creamy and moist. In the States, we eat peanut butter cream pie, scotcheroos, buckeyes (made famous in Ohio), peanut butter brownies, etc.

Peanut Butter Cookies (my grandmother's recipe from Ohio!)

Ingredients:

- 1 cup shortening (kremelta)
- 1 cup caster sugar
- 1 cup brown sugar
- 1 tsp vanilla
- 2 beaten eggs
- 1 cup smooth peanut butter
- 3 cups of flour
- ½ tsp salt (spec of salt as my Grandma would say)
- 1 ½ tsp baking soda

Directions

Cream shortening, sugars , vanilla and eggs together. Stir in peanut butter. Add dry ingredients. Roll into a smooth ball and coat with sugar. Press down on them slightly and bake for 9 min at 180 C. Let them cool for a few minutes, and push a chocolate button or Hershey kiss in the middle.

There are many versions of the Philly cheesesteak out there but a REAL Philly cheesesteak can only come from Philadelphia. Pat's King of Steaks in Philly is the original way to make cheesesteaks with Cheez Wiz! I have located some spray cheese from the American store for this recipe. The key to this recipe is to make sure that the meat, bread and cheese are right! This is one of my favourite foods of all time; now we can make it in New Zealand!

REAL Philly Cheesesteak (Pat's steaks in Philadelphia)

Ingredients:

- 1 red capsicum (pepper)
- 1 green capsicum (pepper)
- 1 onion
- ½ cup of mushrooms (optional)
- Rib Eye steak - This is key!
- Provolone cheese - this can be sourced at Italian restaurants in your area.
    (Substitutes include mozzarella and havarti if you cannot locate provolone)
- Spray cheese (fake cheese)
- Mayo
- Butter
- Heinz Ketchup
- Crusty Italian bread rolls
- Canola oil

Check out my TikTok video on this @kiwiamericans

Directions

Sauté capsicum, mushroom and onion in some oil in a cast iron skillet (if you have one). Set aside. The KEY is to slice the Rib eye meat paper thin, where you can almost see through it.
I take a sharp knife and slice it super thin. An option is to have the butcher do this for you or a sharp cheese slicer can work too. Once the meat is thin, chop it into smaller bits with a knife. Slice the cheese thin as well. You will need to make each sandwich separately.

Start by buttering the bread, toasting it in the pan, and remove. Add more oil to the pan and add chopped meat. Cook for 1 min. Add onion/capsicum/mushroom combo. Take the skillet off the heat once the meat is still pink in the middle. Add cheese slices to the top of the meat while still in the pan. Put mayonnaise on both sides of your bread roll and add the meat/cheese. Top with Ketchup and spray cheese.
Enjoy!

Chilli is a soup recipe commonly made during the colder months of the year. It is very hearty and serves a crowd. Sometimes, at parties, we would have a "chilli dump." Everyone brings a pot of their homemade chili and we dump it all together. There are also chilli competitions at fairs and festivals!

American Chilli - Amazing comfort food!

Ingredients:

- 500g mince
- 1 onion
- 4 cloves garlic
- 1 green capsicum
- 1 TBL chili powder
- 1 TBL cumin
- 2 TBL sugar
- 2 TBL tomato paste
- 1 TBL garlic salt
- 1 tin of tomato puree
- 1 tin of diced tomatoes
- 1 tin of kidney beans drained and rinsed

Toppings
- Sour cream
- Shredded cheese (I like edam on this)
- Macaroni noodles

Directions

Brown mince and add onion, garlic and capsicum on medium heat. Cook for 5 min and add all the spices. Add the rest of the items and let simmer for one hour.

Make sure to crumble some cornbread into the chilli!

This is so easy to make, you will find yourself making it often. It goes with all sorts of meals but we mainly eat it with American Chili! I think it would be good with the Māori boil up or to bring to a "bring a plate" party!

Cornbread (one bowl recipe!)

Ingredients:

- 1 cup all-purpose flour
- 1 cup of cornmeal (polenta)
- 1 cup sugar
- 1 tsp salt
- 3 ½ tsp baking powder
- 1 cup vegetable oil
- 1 large egg
- 1 cup milk

Directions

Grease a small pan and preheat the oven to 200 degrees C. Mix all the dry ingredients together. Make a well in the middle and put all the wet ingredients together. Mix and pour into the pan. Pour into the pan and bake for 15-20 min. Test with a toothpick in the center to see if it comes out clean.

You can find New York and Italian-style pizza in New Zealand, but I have yet to find deep-dish Chicago-style pizza. Our family's favourite deep dish pizza is Lou Malnati's pizza, so I have watched videos, tried a few recipes and come up with a good Lou Malnati's type recipe for you. Last time I was in the States, I liked my version better.

Chicago Deep Dish Pizza (Lou Malnati's style)

Dough
- 3/4 cup+ 2 TBL of lukewarm water
- 1/8 tsp active dry yeast
- ¼ cup vegetable oil
- ¼ cup canola oil
- 2 TBL olive oil
- ¾ tsp salt
- 3 cups of flour (all-purpose)

Let yeast dissolve in the water. Add the rest of the ingredients and mix with an electric mixer. Put in a bowl and cover in olive oil. Let rise for 1-2 hours.

Sauce
- 2 cans of crushed tomatoes
- 3 cloves of garlic
- Olive oil
- 1 1/2 TBL sugar
- 1 tsp Oregano
- 1 tsp Basil (fresh if you have it)

Add olive oil to the pan. Add garlic. Stir in the rest of the ingredients. Simmer for 30 minutes.

Other ingredients
- Mozzarella cheese (ideally in slices or just slice up a large block)
- Parmesan cheese (powdered)
- Meat topping: Italian sausage (Lou Malnati's pizza puts a slab of Italian sausage on their pizza), pepperoni, or plain cheese.
- Polenta (cornmeal)

Heat oven to 215 degrees Celsius. Grease pan and sprinkle bottom and sides with polenta (cornmeal). Roll out the dough and put it in a cheesecake-type springform pan. Make sure the dough goes at least halfway up the side of the pan. Layer with 2-3 layers of mozzarella cheese. Top with meat. Cover in sauce. Sprinkle parmesan cheese on pizza. Bake for 20-30 min. Let sit for 5 minutes before cutting into.

There have been lots of requests for fruit pie, so I thought I would share my Grandmother's cherry pie recipe because I do not see this pie in NZ very often. You can adapt this recipe for all different fruits such as apple, peach, rhubarb etc.

Cherry Pie

Ingredients:

- 1 jar of pitted cherries (drain most of the juice)
- ¾ cup of sugar
- 2 TBL of corn flour
- ½ tsp salt
- ½ tsp almond extract
- Butter crust recipe (outlined in Pumpkin pie recipe)

Directions

Place one pie crust in a 9 in (22 cm) pie pan. Flute edges. Mix all ingredients in a bowl. Pour into pie crust. Roll out the second pie crust and cut it out into a circle that does not come out to the edge of the pie. It is nice when some cherries are showing around the edges. (Sprinkle some sugar on the pie.) Cook at 215 C for 10 min and 180 C for 20 min more. The crust should come out golden brown.

Hint: Always place some aluminium foil on the pie edges to keep them from burning.

Enchiladas are a staple in American Mexican restaurants. This is my favourite recipe that a friend shared with me years ago! I recommend using flour tortillas but you can use corn tortillas as well. If you love Mexican food, then you will love this one.

Chicken Enchiladas – Spicy Honey lime!

Ingredients:

- 4 Chicken breasts cooked/shredded or buy a rotisserie chicken from the deli!
- 1 jar of green salsa verde - I have found at New World
- 8-10 flour tortillas
- 3 cups of Edam and Colby shredded cheese. It's not as good as Monterey Jack, but you can only get it at Costco.

Marinade
- ¾ cup honey
- ½ cup of lime juice
- ½ Tbl chilli powder
- 2 tsp garlic salt
- ½ tsp paprika
- ½ tsp cumin
- ½ tsp chipotle powder
- ¼ tsp pepper
- Dash of cayenne pepper (for extra spice)

Toppings - *Sour cream, avocado, tomato and coriander*

Directions

Add chicken to marinade for 10-20 min. Put a portion of the green salsa at the bottom of the baking dish. Fill tortillas with chicken and some cheese. Roll and place in a large baking dish seam side down.

If you have leftover marinade, mix it with the remaining green salsa and pour over the enchiladas. Cover with the rest of the cheese. Bake at 180 C for 20-30 min. Turn to 200 C and grill for a few minutes to crisp the cheese. Serve hot with toppings.

When we have guests over, we most often make REAL American cheeseburgers! They are different from kiwi burgers as they are pink in the middle, have no beetroot, no egg and always full of flavour. You can use the cheese of your choice but American cheddar cheese is what you would most commonly find on an American burger.

American Cheeseburger

Ingredients:

- 500g to 1kg of premium mince
- 1/3 cup of worcestershire sauce
- 4 cloves of minced garlic
- Salt
- Pepper
- 1-2 egg (I use this if my mince is crumbly)
- Hamburger buns

Toppings: Edam cheese or any cheese that melts well, ketchup, mayo, American mustard, avocado mashed, lettuce, pickle, onion and tomato. Optional - crispy bacon!

Directions

Mix ingredients (except buns) and form patties. Keep them larger than you want as they will shrink on the grill. Add some salt/pepper to the top of the burger.

It is ideal if you can grill on a charcoal grill but a gas grill will also work. Ensure the grill is on *medium heat* as you don't want to cook this all through. You want the burger to be pink in the middle. Add cheese during the last few seconds. Remove the burgers and toast the buns on the grill. Serve with all the toppings to be a proper American burger.

This biscuit is similar to the NZ scone but not exactly the same; it is more flaky and buttery (is that a word?). These can also be served topped with butter/honey along side fried chicken. This is a common breakfast food all over the USA. **Watch this being made on YouTube @ kiwiamericans.**

Buttermilk Biscuits and Gravy

Ingredients

Buttermilk Biscuits:
- 2 1/2 cups self-rising flour (plus extra for flouring your surface)
- 2 teaspoon sugar (optional)
- 1/2 teaspoon kosher salt
- 4 tablespoons vegetable shortening (kremelta)
- 4 tablespoons butter, cut into cubes, chilled
- 1 cup chilled buttermilk, plus 1-2 tablespoons more, if needed*
- 1 tablespoon melted butter (optional, to brush on top of biscuits after baking

Sausage Gravy:
- 500g sage-flavoured pork sausage
- 1/4 cup finely chopped yellow onion
- 6 tablespoons all-purpose flour
- 4 cups whole milk
- 1/4 teaspoon ground nutmeg
- 1/4 teaspoon salt
- 1-2 dashes of Worcestershire sauce
- 1-2 dashes of Tabasco sauce, cayenne pepper, or other hot sauce
- 1-2 tablespoons butter or bacon grease (if needed)

Directions

Preheat oven to 220°C:

Biscuits

Whisk together flour, sugar and salt in a medium-sized bowl. Cut in the shortening and butter with a pastry blender. The mixture should be crumbly. Make a well in the flour mixture, and pour in the buttermilk. With lightly floured hands, turn out the dough onto a lightly-floured surface. Shape and cut with biscuit cutter. Place biscuits on the baking sheet. Reshape

scrap dough and continue cutting. Bake at 220C for 15-18 minutes or until lightly golden brown on top. Brush the tops of the biscuits with melted butter.

Gravy

Brown the sausage and add the onion. Add in the spices and flour. Slowly pour in the milk. Let simmer at medium heat until the gravy thickens. Pour gravy over biscuits! Enjoy :)

*see the pancake recipe to make this homemade.

Meatloaf, a typical American comfort food, has been a weekly staple food in the USA. This is why I included it as my family still loves it. We always serve it with mashed potatoes and veggies :)

Meatloaf

Ingredients:

- 1 kg of premium mince
- 1 med onion finely chopped
- 2 large eggs
- 3 garlic cloves minced
- 3 Tbsp ketchup
- 3 Tbsp fresh parsley finely chopped
- 3/4 cup breadcrumbs
- ¼ cup milk
- 1 ½ tsp salt or to taste
- 1 ½ tsp Oregano
- ¼ tsp ground black pepper
- ½ tsp ground paprika

Meatloaf Sauce Ingredients:

3/4 cup ketchup
1 ½ tsp white vinegar
2 ½ Tbsp brown sugar
1 tsp garlic salt
¼ tsp ground black pepper

Directions

Line a loaf pan with parchment paper or cooking spray. Preheat the oven to 180 C.

In a large bowl, add all of the ingredients for the meatloaf. Mix well to combine. Add meat to the loaf pan, gently press meat down and shape evenly and bake meatloaf at 180°C for 40 minutes.

In a small bowl, mix all of the ingredients together for the sauce. Spread the sauce over meatloaf then return to oven and bake additional 15-20 minutes. Rest meatloaf 10 minutes before slicing. Drizzle with baking juices from the pan.

I get the question: What is ranch dressing and what do Americans put it on? Well, I have heard your requests and produced a homemade recipe for Ranch dressing. This can be used to dip raw veggies in, on salad, chicken nuggets and pretty much anything and everything!

Buttermilk Ranch Dressing

Ingredients:

- 1/2 cup mayonnaise
- 1/2 cup sour cream
- 1/2 cup buttermilk
- 3/4 teaspoon dried dill weed
- 1/2 teaspoon dried parsley
- 1/2 teaspoon dried chives
- 1/4 teaspoon onion flakes
- 1/2 teaspoon garlic salt
- 1/4 teaspoon fine sea salt
- 1/8 teaspoon pepper
- freshly squeezed lemon

Directions

Whisk together the mayo, sour cream and buttermilk until smooth. Add the spices and whisk until combined. Add the lemon and whisk again. Pour into a jar and chill in the refrigerator until ready to serve. This dressing will keep nicely in the refrigerator for up to a week. Enjoy!